MW01616540

PROTOCOL

Restoring Honor And Divine Order To The House Of God

Spiritual
PROTOCOL
Restoring Honor And Divine Order To The House Of God

Dr. Keira Taylor-Banks

EXPANDING YOUR VISION
PUBLISHERS

VIRGINIA BEACH, VIRGINIA

Published by Expanding Your Vision Publishers

Expanding Your Vision Nonfiction
Expanding Your Vision Publishers

Printed in the United States of America

First Expanding Your Vision Publishers Printing: July 2009
ISBN: 978-0-9817488-5-6

Cover design by Stephen Blackmon.

Dedication

*This book is dedicated to the faithful and devoted pastors
around the globe who have given their lives
to lovingly care for God's people.*

Contents

Foreword

.$\mathscr{I}$t is undoubtedly a great privilege and an honor
to pen the foreword to my wife's latest book, "*Spiritual
Protocol*," to The Body of Christ. In this masterpiece on
the modus operandi for divine order in the Kingdom
realm, Dr. Keira delineates with distinct clarity, the critical
aspects of establishing and maintaining order and honor,
not only within the corporate body, but in particular the
local house of God.

Dr. Keira Banks, an anointed vessel of God who
faithfully serves her family, her church and the Kingdom of
God, seeks nothing more than to prophetically encourage
and challenge believers to rightfully take their place to
inspire the world with the Kingdom mandate. She flows
in the Apostolic and Prophetic anointing with exceptional
grace and fervor fulfilling her multifaceted assignment
meticulously. She is a precious and sparkling jewel to our
family and a Spiritual Mother worthy of respect and honor

11

in the Kingdom of God.

I recommend this book not just because it has excellent, thoroughly researched spiritual and biblical content but because I have known her to live-out her teachings. Beyond the veil of this talented and gifted writer, talk show host, creative and prolific orator, there is a person of integrity and utmost honor. Having served together in pastoral ministry for over 20 years she brings a unique perspective to this overlooked and maligned subject matter.

I encourage Pastors and fellow co-laborers to follow these guidelines, precept upon precept and you will establish the order, honor, and respect that God desires for you and your congregation. In doing so I decree that fresh oil shall be released from the head (pastors) to the beard (leadership) to the skirts of the garments (fellowship).

Enjoy!!

Bishop Steven W. Banks, General Overseer
Living Waters International Alliance
Newport News Virginia

Introduction

I am writing *Spiritual Protocol: Restoring Honor and Divine Order to The House of God* to help God's people enter into a greater understanding of the thought and intent of God, as it relates to order and Spiritual Protocol in the local church, as well as the Body of Christ. Too often, leaders and members within a congregation engage in serious violations of protocol, sometimes intentionally and often unintentionally, which renders a congregation dysfunctional and incapable of executing the Kingdom of God realm. When there is disorder in a church, the Apostolic and Prophetic anointing are compromised to strife, contention, and egregious displays of egotism. Restoring the Kingdom of God realm is tantamount to restoring order. God is a God of Divine Order. His Kingdom of Light is a glorious and ordered realm.

God's House is a house of love, light, prayer, and order. All relationships in the house of God should reflect

13

and support these conditions. The local church is a unique social setting, and in any social situation it is understood that offences and difficulties will arise. It is naïve to expect anything else. The best of marriages endure conflict from time to time. In the best of families, there is sibling rivalry, conflict, and betrayal that must be resolved.

The House of God should be thought of as a Spiritual Family with its varied players and characters (John 19:25-27). Even as conflicts and situations bring about challenges in any family structure, families manage to hold together, to forgive, and to resolve issues, because the family is built upon the foundation of love and mutual respect. In the same manner, the local church should teach and demonstrate the principles of Spiritual Protocol within the context of the Spiritual Family, as a defense against the hidden conspiracy of the enemy to bring disruption and dishonor to The Church and therefore, people of the Christian faith.

Over the twenty years I have served in Christian ministry, I find that the most egregious violators of Spiritual Protocol are leaders who have been tasked with delegated authority within a local congregation. We find a disruptive pattern where leadership at some point in time casts-off an attitude of submission and begins to rival ordained leadership. Oftentimes, an over-inflated ego and spiritual pride sets in and although they may engage tasks obediently, their hearts are full of secret criticism, contention, and competition.

Delegated leaders should understand that their primary role is to love, support, undergird, and promote the vision of the set man and woman of God. God operates and dwells in a realm of Divine Order. Any actions, behaviors, or attitudes that do not reflect supportive love, kindness, and honor extended to pastors, and from member to member, is a direct violation of Spiritual Protocol and a breach in God's precisely ordered Kingdom.

The primary satanic deception is that the organized church is a democracy where each individual has their say and opinion. If this were the case, a church would remain in a perpetual state of confusion, immobilization, and could never release the Kingdom mandate or mission under these circumstances. The Bible teaches that The Church is a theocracy. This means that the government of the church is Biblically ordered and commanded by God. In a theocracy, there is rule by God through Biblical patterns and precepts. There is God ordained rule in the Kingdom, and then there is man-made rule and government. The Hiscox Guide for rule or the Robert's Rules of Order, which introduced democratic rule in churches, is not Biblical governmental rule for the House of God. Congregationally run churches are not on sound Biblical footing.

The House of God is a Theocracy and not a democracy. While democratic government is treasured in

American society, it is a structure that cannot be forced upon God, His House, or His Divinely Ordered Kingdom realm. Theocratic rule means that God speaks to and through ordained Five-Fold leadership, namely pastors called to serve the local church. The vision for the House of God is downloaded to pastoral leadership. The vision flows from the top down and not the bottom-up. God never elected a congregation to run His house, neither did He anoint or equip trustees or deacons to guide the vision of the House. This is the responsibility of those men and women carrying any combination of governmental anointing found in Ephesians 4:11, 12 (apostles, prophets, evangelists, pastors, and teachers). In the Kingdom of God, the anointing determines where governmental rule will rest.

Biblical governmental order is an ordained man and woman of God who are couriers of the vision, mission, and supernatural intelligence necessary to rule in any given local church. They are representative of the Kingdom of God realm and order established with the first couple in the Book of Genesis (Genesis 1:26, 27). In Genesis, we find both Adam and Eve received the impartation, the empowerment, the commanded blessing, and supernatural intelligence to embody Kingdom of God government and rule. The command to have dominion is the command to rule in the Kingdom of God domain. In Genesis chapter one, Eve cannot be extracted of the text, therefore, she is

Adam's counterpart and equal partner in rulership. Later in Genesis, we see Abraham given a sphere of governmental rule and authority as 'Father of Many Nations' and Sarah also is given an equal, but different sphere of governmental rule and authority as 'Mother of Many Nations' (Genesis 17:5, 16). Therefore, in Apostolic and Prophetic Houses, the wife of the set man cannot be suppressed and dismissed, as it relates to governmental rule in the House of God, and therefore the Kingdom realm. The myth perpetuated by religion is that redemptive work is the work of men alone. In this hour of Apostolic Reformation, the place of the woman is to be restored.

The Biblical precedent for governmental rule does not include boards and committees dictating to pastoral authority. God ordains pastors to lead and govern churches (Ephesians 4:11, 12). Deacons, trustees, and all other leadership are called to conduct tasks of servant-hood, excluding governmental rule (Acts 6:1-7). Elders are called to engage a variety of administrative duties, including delegated teaching and/or pastoral tasks (I Tim. 5:15, James 5:14).

The problem for the organized church is that religion has created man-made structures for government that are always characterized by strife and dysfunction. I assert that these structures are unbiblical, even though they have been around for many, many years and we are very familiar with them. Apostolic and Prophetic people must embrace the

17

order of God. This means that the vision and anointing comes from the head (Psalm 133:2). The congregation cannot be the source of the vision or government in the house of God. The congregation is called and anointed to dutifully and faithfully execute the vision.

Spiritual Protocol is a guide to assist leaders and members of churches through successful transitions in their service in the house of God. Serving a man and woman of God in ministry is a joy and an honor and never a battle for territory. Humility and loyalty are the marks of anointed delegated leadership and authority in the local church. Delegated leaders must understand that serving others is a prerequisite to obtaining their own ministry assignment:

> *"And if ye have not been faithful in that which is another man's, who shall give you that which is your own?" (Luke 16:12)*

PROTOCOL:
Restoring Honor And Divine Order To The House Of God

Spiritual Protocol

Spiritual Protocol refers to the honor, preference, and respect due to those in spiritual authority within the local church, and is extended to those advanced offices, as well as all delegated leadership within the Body of Christ. Spiritual Protocol is one of the hallmarks of an Apostolic and Prophetic house (ministry). When Spiritual Protocol is honored, the Prophetic Dimension is manifested and accessed within a congregation. When Spiritual Protocol is not understood or enforced, the authentic Apostolic and Prophetic Dimension is forfeited to the counterfeit, and more often than not, it is non-existent.

Spiritual Protocol is the Kingdom of God code of conduct reflecting the honor, respect, and deference due *at all times* to those spiritual leaders of higher rank. The Kingdom of the Living God is a realm of divine order and authority. Lines of protocol must be obeyed and respected, bringing God the honor due His name in His house. While it is true that all of God's children share an uncontested spiritual equality, an individual identified of lesser rank must yield to the individual of higher rank. Since the Kingdom of God is an ordered Kingdom, spiritual ranking then is a matter of priority and not an issue of equality in any social sense.

In the military, clear lines of authority and protocol are well established. An army enlisted man knows the deference and subordination that is due an officer or general. These lines of authority and respect cannot be violated. In this manner, The Kingdom of God is a well ordered and hierarchical realm. The priority here is the sovereign command of the King. The command and authority of the King must rest upon the uncontested and unquestioned execution by those within assigned ranks. The Kingdom of God rests upon the sole authority of Christ who is under the command of God Almighty. Even as Christ is submitted to the will and command of His Heavenly Father, believers within the ranks of the Kingdom must reflect this same perfection of unity, submission, agreement, and execution.

Christians must first recognize that we are a people under authority. To meet God is to meet His authority. Individuals who say they know God, but cannot yield to His earthly representative authority *have not met God.* The fact is that God chooses men and women to represent Him in the earth. Often, these are ascension gifts that represent extraordinary Spiritual Dimensions of power (Ephesians 4:11, 12). These gifts are to be honored, respected, and protected. Faith in God and our understanding of authority are linked (Matthew 8:5-10).We cannot release authentic faith in God if we have not ascribed to His full authority in our lives.

HONOR

Kingdom people are able to receive spiritual impartation from ordained leadership because of their adherence to codes of honor, kindness, and respect. Spiritual impartation flows freely when *honor* is in place. The New Testament indicates that in certain places, Jesus could do no mighty work as a result of unbelief and the levels of dishonor present (Mark 6:5). In churches where Spiritual Protocol is not in effect, very little spiritual impartation is present (although dynamic and revelatory preaching may be operative), and disrespect and confusion reign. The Prophet Malachi declares God's heart on this vital Kingdom principle:

> *"A son honoureth his father, and a servant his*
> *master: if then I be a father, where is mine honour?*
> *And if I be a master, where is my fear? Saith the Lord*

of hosts unto you, O priests, that despise my name.
And ye say, Wherein have we despised thy name?"
(Malachi 1:6)

One cannot claim sonship or connection with their leaders if a system and the practice of honor is not firmly in place. Honor is a sign that an individual values the expression of God in His representatives. To honor individuals does not take away from the person ascribing honor; it actually proves the believer's humility and level of maturity. To honor your pastor does not mean that you are without worth or significance. In every way you are equal to your pastors; however, because there are uniquely potent dimensions of power resident in your pastors, this alone requires that you handle them with love and care. To honor another individual means that you are recognizing *the life of God* within them. As we honor others, God Himself is honored. Significant and life-changing withdrawals are made when we honor significant others. It is my practice to honor the elderly, the Mothers in our church, and all those who are serving. Honor is not simply reserved for pastors. As believers, we are to honor the God in everyone, since God has chosen to express Himself through each and every uniquely created individual that bears His name. As it relates to honor this is what Jesus taught:

"He that receiveth you receiveth me; and he that receiveth me receiveth him that sent me.

He that receiveth a prophet in the name of a prophet shall receive a prophet's reward; and he that receiveth a righteous man in the name of a righteous man shall receive a righteous man's reward.

And whosoever shall give to drink unto one of these little ones a cup of cold water only in the name of a disciple, verily I say unto you, he shall in no wise lose his reward." (Matthew 10:40-42)

In this text from The Gospel of Matthew, Jesus is teaching that honor runs the full spectrum of our relationships. Here, Jesus lists four categories 1) the honor of God, 2) the honor of Five-Fold gifts (prophets), 3) the honor of righteous men, and 4) the honor of the least of these (widows, children, orphans, and the outcast). Honor must flow throughout all of our relationships in the House of God. This is a picture of true Spiritual Protocol and the love of God as expressed by true believers. Spiritual Protocol is rooted in an authentic love for God, which translates into an unselfish love for His people.

Jesus lamented over the lack of honor amongst his own people:

"Is not this the carpenter, the son of Mary, the brother of James, and Joses, and of Juda, and Simon?

And are not his sisters here with us? And they were offended at him.

But Jesus said, unto them, A prophet is not without honor, but in his own country, and among his own kin, and in his own house.

And he could there do no mighty work, save that he laid his hands upon a few sick folk, and healed them.

And he marveled because of their unbelief."
(Mark 6:3-6)

RECOVERING RELATIONSHIPS

Prophetic people must know and obey lines of Spiritual Protocol in the Kingdom of God. A violation of protocol can constitute a damaging and costly error and setback for one desiring to do ministry and to please God. Since God is a God of relationship, when an error in protocol is made it is important that the violation is acknowledged and the violator is *humble and wise enough* to repair whatever damage was done (Matthew 10:40-42, I Sam. 9:6-9, Malachi 1:6). Reconciling relationships is critical as one engages critical Kingdom assignments.

Jesus encouraged reconciliation, purity, and honor in relationships (Matthew 5:22-24, 7: 1-5). When there has been a breach of honor, the way to restore a relationship with a spiritual father/ mother or brother/ sister is to offer a verbal apology to clear the air, or to present a gift as an act of honor. Violations of spiritual protocol do not magically disappear. Even after a number of years have passed, it may be critical to destiny to restore an offense, to address a misunderstanding, or to smooth out a disagreement, ensuring that spiritual relationships remain intact (2 Samuel 21:1-3). Of course, this requires *humility and* the *absence of spiritual pride.*

As we understand spiritual ranking more clearly, we must understand that a ministry title does not give one instant spiritual ranking. Experience, maturity, and divine appointment are what give the ranking. Therefore, all pastors, bishops, apostles, prophets, etc. are not equally ranked. Titles in and of themselves are not always a true indication of spiritual ranking. Rank is known by God, discerned by the mature, and is given expression through ministry. The principle is to yield when you discern that you are in the presence of *someone greater than yourself in spiritual order.* In the Book of Genesis, we find Abraham honoring Melchizedek, believed to be the pre-incarnate Christ, *with tithes of all* (Genesis 14:18-20). As great as Abraham was in his high appointment and calling, *he found someone greater than himself,* and the Bible says he honored this Melchizedek, King of Salem. In this instance, there was an exchange made. Melchizedek blessed and released great spiritual impartation into Abraham's life, and Abraham responded by offering his tithe to this great man.

If a pastor does not believe that there is anyone of a greater spiritual ranking, then he or she is a victim of his or her own spiritual pride and deception. Why is this? The Kingdom of God is an ordered Kingdom. If you are not found amongst the ranks of the Kingdom of Light, then how can you make impact without the backing and authority of God's ordained order? Accepting one's position amongst a host of other Kingdom operatives is a matter of personal humility. Egotism has no place amongst Kingdom ranking.

A Kingdom Of Love, Light, Prayer, And Order

LOVE

In what manner can we adequately describe God's glorious Kingdom? The Kingdom of God is summed-up in one word, and that is love. Love is the Kingdom of God in demonstration. The Church is enamored with the *message* of the Kingdom. We *sing* the message, we *shout over* the message, and we *study* the message obsessively. Somehow, we are short on its demonstration. The fact is that The Church is called to be *the demonstration and embodiment of the love of God* in the earth. Where there is the absence of love, then there is no Kingdom manifestation or realm. God is love. Any discussion of Spiritual Protocol would not be complete or consistent without a discussion of love. Everything in God's ordered Kingdom begins and ends with love. If it is not a loving act, a loving church, a loving thought, or a loving Word,

29

then check the source.

Over the years, I have had my challenges with understanding God's non-judgmental love. As a pastor, I have truly grown in understanding God as love. As I embrace love and its Kingdom mandate, I am better equipped to love God's people. I have learned that to pastor a people is to serve them and to accept each and every one for the jewels that they are, as well as for the flaws that they present. I trust that the people I serve can accept my flaws. I have learned that all humans are hopelessly flawed, and the Bible does not hide this fact. I have learned that God is a God of relationships, and that the most mature believers are those who wisely manage their relationships with love. Love cannot fail. Love is the ultimate answer to whatever the problem, and love trumps all. There is no law, legality, policy, or Bible doctrine that trumps the law of love. Jesus taught on the topic of love:

> *"Master, which is the great commandment in the law?*
> *Jesus said unto him, Thou shalt love the Lord thy God with all thy heart, and with all thy soul, and with all thy mind.*
> *This is the first and great commandment.*
> *And the second is like unto it, Thou shalt love thy neighbor as thyself.*
> ***On these two commandments hang all the law and the prophets.*** *(Matthew 22:36-40)*

Unfortunately, there are many churches that do not exhibit love in any way, shape, or form. These are normally congregationally run churches where the pastor is tolerated and the pastor's wife is dismissed. Typically, these churches are stuck in the muck and the mire of religious tradition, and are grievously dysfunctional. There is strife, contention, and displays of arrogance. There are continuous in-fighting and outrageous performances of ignorance, backward thinking, and back-woods thinking. I have no idea how sane people who say they love God remain in these structures. If I had to drive 45 minutes (as many believers do) to attend a loving, orderly, and sane church I would do it!

I do not believe that a pastor called to serve God can release the full weight of his or her anointing or assignment in these loveless dens of iniquity, disguised as houses of worship. *My advice is that you should run for your life!* If you are a member in a dysfunctional house, just know that your sincere desire to be fully released in your assignment and gifting cannot take place there. If you are a pastor, know that God is waiting for you to get a glimpse of the scope and depth of His glorious Kingdom of God realm, which does not include structures that in fact are in conflict with Christ (Matthew Chapters 21 and 23). For pastors with a desire to do a great work for God, be advised that your vision and desire cannot come forth in the midst of on-going confusion. The continuous subjection of your wife and family to the stress, disappointment, betrayals, and constant attacks are not worth the pittance they are paying you.

The Kingdom realm has nothing to do with loveless and lifeless religious structures. They are totally irrelevant to the Kingdom of God mandate in the earth. These churches exist only to serve themselves and to torment the uninformed individuals who worship there. God is not in institutionalized confusion. The Holy Spirit cannot rule in an atmosphere of gossip, slander, hate, and malicious intent from uninspired individuals who masquerade as Christians. You may be singing there, but singing to whom? You may be shouting, but shouting for what? The glory of God has abandoned these obsolete structures and written ICHABOD upon the door posts. (I Samuel 4:21)

LIGHT

The Kingdom of God is a realm of splendid light. God is light (I John 1:5-7). His Kingdom is made of pure and brilliant Light. The first command was for darkness to be disrupted by light (Genesis 1:3). Light reproves, light exposes, light infiltrates darkness, and exists to shine and to show forth Christ in all of His glory. The Church is to walk in light, to embody light, and to release light in the earth. The fact is that if we have light, we have illumination; if we have illumination we then have revelation; if we have revelation, then we are enlightened, and if we are now enlightened, we are delivered from our enemy, which is darkness and ignorance. The fact is that the revelatory Word is light (2 Corinthians 4:4), and *knowledge* of the Word brings light (2 Corinthians 4:6).

Our churches should be filled with love and light. If you have love, then you have light. The assignment of the church is to embody light. When light is not present in a church, there is the absence of vision and visionary instinct. When light is not present, there is no revelatory teaching, only a repackaging of the old worn-out teachings. When light is not present, there is no insight for oversight; there is no depth of perception or prophetic sight. Jesus taught on the topic of light:

> *"Ye are the light of the world. A city that is set on a hill cannot be hid.*
>
> *Neither do men light a candle, and put it under a bushel, but on a candlestick; and it giveth light unto all that are in the house.*
>
> *Let your light so shine before men, that they may see your good works, and glorify your Father which is in heaven." (Matthew 5:14-17)*

Crass ignorance is the enemy of light. When we remain ignorant to the movement and the ways of God it is because we choose to remain ignorant. God's Word promises that we will discover Him when we seek after Him with all of our hearts (Jeremiah 29:11-13). God is not playing hide and seek with those who love him. God has made His Kingdom intent, clear, and visible. In this age of information technology and high speed access on the information highway, if people choose to live in the darkness of religious tradition, while rejecting the Kingdom of God realm of splendid light and love, then this is a conscious choice.

PRAYER

The Kingdom realm is a supernatural realm where extraordinary things manifest as a result of prayer. Jesus said, *'My house shall be called the house of prayer'* (Matthew 21:13; Mark 11:17; Luke 19:46). Therefore, in effective churches, Intercessory Ministry is the primary ministry that expresses the core value of the community of believers. Through prayer, we gain access to the mind, the agenda, and the heartbeat of God. As a believing community, congregations should be taught that Intercession and redemptive outcomes are vitally linked. Leaders in an Apostolic and Prophetic House are trained and expected to participate in prayer.

There are two categories of prayer that are critical

to the success of the work of the ministry: 1) private devotional prayer and 2) Corporate Intercession. Private devotion is what every believer is expected to engage as a part of their personal spiritual regimen. Believers are taught to listen, to wait, to worship, to be still, to sing, to confess, to decree, and to proclaim in the presence of God. Personal prayer develops the soul. The soul (the mind, will, and the emotion) is the unruly, untamed, and often unchecked part of the believer that goes left when God says to go right. Private and consistent prayer silences the raging of the ego that demands attention and resists God's authority. Without private prayer and devotion, the believer is like a ship without a sail. I would not follow any leader who does not engage an active and vibrant, private prayer life.

Corporate Intercession is vital to growing a strong, vibrant church that is operative in Divine Order and Kingdom of God strategies. Corporate Intercession is prayer that includes the local body of believers. In a house of order, leaders lead. As it relates to Corporate Intercession, authentic leadership connects with this core value of the house, and is therefore ready and available to seek the presence of God through prayer. Corporate Intercession is not an option. Serious business is conducted in the realm of the spirit in prayer. A Kingdom of God culture and mindset cannot be established outside of Corporate Intercession. If a people cannot be governed in prayer, then they have forfeited their leadership of others.

Christians cannot expect to express the purposes and intent of God by sheer will, creativity, and human thought alone. The Bible teaches that we must ask for the will of God through prayer (Matthew 16:18, 19, 18: 19, 21:22; Luke 11:9; John 14:14, 15:16, 16:23-26). Things just don't happen, and Christians are not *to just sit by passively waiting for God* to do what He will do. The Bible teaches that God has delegated the earth to man. Man, as God's delegated authority, is commanded to act as God's representatives in the earth. We are called to make incredible things happen through prayer! Prayer is access to spiritual dimensions and portals of awesome power! In this earthly domain, prayer becomes the womb and the birthing channel through which the extraordinary and supernatural manifests. A people who have neglected prayer have abandoned The Almighty God.

ORDER

Divine Order is vital to the Kingdom of God reality, realm, and system. The Kingdom of God is not manifested through knowledge and wishful thinking. The Kingdom rests upon the foundation of Divine Order. Everything about God's Kingdom is ordered. The Bible teaches that the angelic kingdom is ranked and ordered, the stars that are showcased at night are represented in a strategic order, and the cosmos itself is in orderly arrangement and alignment. Every grain of sand and blade of grass is properly arranged, assembled, and is ordered in God's creation. And yet, we still believe that disorder is acceptable in our churches and fellowships.

Individuals come into the alignment of Divine Order, because their hearts are pure and they have a desire to please Almighty God. Those with hidden, and not so hidden, agendas are operative in a spirit of lust of the flesh and carnality. In Apostolic and Prophetic churches, peace and order are essential to the function and the climate within the House of God, and those that create confusion should be rebuffed by those in authority. The Bible teaches that contention, confusion, and strife are not of God, but has a satanic source that must be identified and prohibited. The Apostle Paul instructed concerning the disorderly:

> *"For, brethren, ye have been called unto liberty; only use not liberty for an occasion to the flesh, but by love serve one another.*
>
> *For all the law is fulfilled in one word, even in this; Thou shalt love thy neighbor as thyself.*
>
> *But if ye bite and devour one another, take heed that ye be not consumed one of another.*
>
> *This I say then, Walk in the Spirit, and ye shall not fulfil the lust of the flesh." (Galatians 5:13-16)*

Operating in Divine Order simply means that each believer yields the right of way to others, particularly those in authority. In a house of order, kindness, forgiveness, peace, and reconciliation rule. When there is order, disputes are settled peaceably and conflicts are resolved privately in the spirit of love and meekness. When order is present, malicious gossip is shut-down and offenses do not spread like wildfire. Divine Order means that individuals are committed to demonstrating The Fruit of the Spirit, as expressed in the New Testament (Galatians 5:22, 23):

"But the fruit of the spirit is love, joy, peace, long-suffering, gentleness, goodness, faith,
Meekness, temperance: against such there is no law." (Galatians 5:22, 23)

Spiritual Pride

*I*t is very difficult for many Christians to accept spiritual ranking, since most are so full of spiritual pride. Spiritual pride is a huge problem and an undetected condition in many. We preach, teach, shout, jump and judge others, all in the attitude of unchecked *spiritual pride*. Spiritual pride is the most damaging, deceptive, and dangerous condition for the believer. The greatest of sin may not be the obvious sexual sins we love to call out. But the Bible declares pride to be an abomination and the most egregious of sins (Proverbs 6:16). It is most often hidden and concealed, going undetected and therefore unchecked for many years. Many seasoned believers get ensnared by pride, oblivious to its nastiness and destructive outcomes in relationships. Oftentimes, the pride of demonstrated gifting and anointing cause one to cast-off humility and *to see oneself as equal* with those we should remain heart-submitted and committed to. Pride is an affront to God.

Pride is in conflict with the Kingdom of God command for *humility.*

1. **Pride is a mark of the children of the Kingdom of Darkness and not the children of light.**

   *"He beholdeth all high things: he is a king over all **the children of pride**." (Job 41:34, speaking of Leviathan, the personification of pride)*

2. **Pride leaves God out of the equation, as it relates to honor and respect in relationships in the House of God.**

   *"The wicked, through the pride of his countenance, will not seek after God: **God is not in all his thoughts.**" (Psalm 10:4)*

3. **Pride is manifested in strife and contentious speech.**

   *"Thou shalt hide them in the secret of thy presence from the pride of man: thou shalt keep them secretly in a pavilion from **the strife of tongues**". (Psalm 31:20)*
   *"Only by pride cometh **contention**: but with the well-advised is wisdom." (Proverbs 13:10)*

*"**For the sin of their mouth** and the words of their lips let them even be taken in their pride: and for cursing and lying which they speak."* (Psalm 59:12)

*"In the mouth of the foolish is **a rod of pride**: but the lips of the wise shall preserve them."* (Proverbs 14:3)

4.   Pride and physical violence are connected.

"Therefore pride compasseth them about as a chain; violence covereth them as a garment." (Psalm 73:6)

"When pride cometh, then cometh shame: but with the lowly is wisdom" (Proverbs 11:2)

5.   Pride manifests before major destiny detours are made.

*"**Pride** goeth before **destruction**, and a **haughty spirit** before a **fall**."* (Proverbs 16:18)

*"But if ye will not hear it, **my soul shall weep in secret places for your pride**; and mine eye shall*

weep sore, and run down with tears, because the
Lord's flock is carried away captive."
(Jeremiah 13:17)

"For all that is in the world, the lust of the flesh,
*and the lust of the eyes, and the **pride of life**, is*
not of the Father, but is of the world."
(I John 2:16)

6. **Young believers and those new to leadership are**
    more vulnerable to pride than others.

    *"Not a novice (beginner), lest being **lifted up**
    with pride he fall into the condemnation of the
    devil." (I Timothy 3:6, emphasis mine)*

7. **Spiritual Pride has its origin in the fall of Satan.**

    "How art thou fallen from heaven, O Lucifer,
    son of the morning! how art thou cut down to the
    ground, which didst weaken the nations!
    *For thou hast said in thine heart, **I will** ascend*
    *into heaven, **I will** exalt my throne above the*
    *stars of God: **I will** sit also upon the mount of the*
    congregation, in the sides of the north:

I will ascend above the heights of the clouds; *I
will be like the most High*.
*Yet thou shalt be brought down to hell, to the sides
of the pit." (Isaiah 14:12-15)*

Spiritual pride is easily detected. These are the 5 C's
of pride.

1. **Comparison** – A believer who should remain
    submitted to a pastor begins to spend an inordinate
    amount of time comparing themselves to their leader.
    This is where often the leader will begin to emulate
    their pastor in many inappropriate ways. Emulation
    is a sign that the individual wanting to 'be like'
    their leader is secretly competing. Not having fully
    formulated their own 'identity', the insecure leader
    begins to dress like and speak like and sometimes shop
    like their pastor. Although this may look innocent,
    it can be a dangerous spiritual state where the pastor's
    identity is illegally and secretly stolen in hopes of
    gaining their anointing. This all begins with secret
    inordinate comparison.

    Leaders will often begin comparing their speaking and
    delivery style with that of their pastors. They will begin
    to take inordinate amounts of mental space thinking

of their level of influence with the congregation in relation to their pastors. They begin comparing spiritual gifting. They begin to think that they can do a thing better or with greater precision. *They begin to secretly disagree with many pastoral decisions.* This is comparison at work, leading to greater deception and damage in the relationship between pastor and leader.

Leaders serving pastors should refrain from comparisons. This is unwise and leads to dangerous spiritual outcomes. A rule in Spiritual Protocol is that submitted leaders accept that they are a guest in someone else's house. Whatever the order, policies, or decisions, leaders are not responsible for them, *nor do they have any say in executive matters.* In all executive level/administrative matters or concerns it is best to *have no opinion.* Stay out of matters that do not concern you. Allow the pastors to pastor, and remember only they are accountable before God. The moment a negative opinion of a decision is formed, a door has been opened inviting *the spirit of pride.*

2. **Criticism** – Criticism is a sign that an individual has been given over to pride. Negative speech and secret criticism is rampant in many churches. I have often detected this spirit by way of discernment. Criticism

means that a leader is unsubmitted in his or her heart. They may be serving wonderfully and engaging acts of obedience, but their hearts may be harboring secret offense or a sense of superiority.

Criticism is primarily conducted in secret. This means that the leader has to wear two faces. He or she must put on a mask in church, attempting to cover the disfigurement of their spiritual state. Criticism is the voice of spiritual pride. When the leader cannot execute because their heart is full of criticism, often you get a level of sabotage taking place in their ministry assignment. Rather than working in harmony and unity with the vision, they secretly hope the assignment fails, and are oftentimes plotting its demise.

I do not keep critical people around very long, because it leads to disloyalty and betrayal. Once the spirit of pride is detected, I remove the individual from their post. A ministry cannot flourish when leaders are secretly harboring disagreement. Contentious words spoken in private leave heaviness in the spiritual atmosphere. This counters the free flow of creative and dynamic anointing necessary to release assignments. I cannot afford to have the free flow of anointing blocked by individuals who secretly oppose pastoral government. In Apostolic houses, leaders serve at the pleasure of the pastor or set man or woman. Like Donald Trump, I do not give an individual a second chance to be disloyal. In this regard, I am not concerned with filling up seats with disgruntled and disloyal folk. I am more concerned with filling seats with those who will lend their faith and loyalty to support pastoral vision. Moreover, the health of a ministry is much more important than its size. You do not need the critical and disloyal in your inner circle or leadership ranks.

3. **Competition** - Competition is a monster. Competition is a progression from comparison, to criticism, and then finally, visible competition begins to manifest. This is when the leader has thrown down the gauntlet and has decided to rival and challenge you openly. Often, this rivalry is manifested in subtle ways you may think are harmless in the beginning. If a leader has to shop where you shop and buy the labels you buy and drive what you drive in a determined and desperate manner, then you are dealing with spiritual pride, which has manifested itself in competition.

Competition is a rivalry. It begins subtly and progresses into the nasty and divisive manifestation that it truly is. Often, leaders will flex and self-promote through the ministry assignments given to them, attempting to prove that *I am your equal, because I can do what you do equally well.* This secret notion is misinformed, since the Kingdom is ordered and *is operative by authority and rank* and not by gifting (I Cor. 12:28). So, while it may be true you can preach the doors off the hinges of the church; *this does not make you equal in rank to your pastors.* An anointed pastor will recognize your gifting, support you, and provide growth opportunities. However, they are not obligated to do so. The pulpit is given to the set man or woman and they are under no obligation to give anyone the mic. Therefore, a humble leader will understand the importance of maintaining a heart-submission, and refrain from engaging any egotistical displays of grandstanding out of secret competition. It is important that developing leaders remain under authority while they are serving others.

4. **Covetousness** – Covetousness is a progression of competition. This is a manifestation of pride that demands that *I have what you have.* Covetousness is based on the perverted belief that the greatest of God's gifts are material. It is desperate and dangerous and is based on the notion that *if I have the things you have,* then we are equal in spiritual ranking. Covetousness

is a grasping and a grabbing for material things. Covetousness is borne out of a mental and emotional competition that is egotistical and remains deeply hidden in the psyche, *driving* individuals to want things as a way of proving their own worth. It is a type of '*keeping up with the Jones'* that begins to develop when God begins to bless pastoral leadership. There is such a fixation on the pastors that to prove standing and status in the ministry, individuals governed by pride will make major purchases *they cannot afford.* There are two things happening here: 1) In the minds of those governed by pride, this proves social and organizational status and 2) This is often an outgrowth of secret competition with pastors, since pastors are often loved, admired, and envied *all at the same time.*

5. **Contention** – Contention is the final and ugliest stage of manifested spiritual pride. This is when the gloves come off and individuals just let it all hang out. Attitudes and offenses that were deeply hidden are revealed, and strife begins to take place. Contention is heart-breaking to watch and to experience. This is when individuals will conspire, hold illegal and secret meetings, tell lies, back-stab, and attempt to scandalize pastoral leadership, because they feel wronged when they are corrected or exposed.

Individuals full of spiritual pride cannot be governed. They have slipped back into carnality and cannot be located. The problem here is that if they are left within your congregation they can cause great damage by intentionally poisoning others with their offense. Contention is something that must be addressed by pastors in authority. One cannot ignore individuals loose in the congregation, spewing dirt and lies and offense. Pastors should meet with such individuals and remove them from any ministry responsibilities, while seeking peaceful and loving reconciliation. If reconciliation is not possible and disruptions continue, the pastor has the authority to ask these disgruntled leaders to pray about finding another place to worship, since they will not be permitted to remain in the fellowship operating in *the spirit of offense and contention*. Pastors cannot be fearful of maintaining order and peace in their churches, since God ultimately will hold them accountable for the climate within their congregation.

Submission

Submission is tantamount to a discussion of Spiritual Protocol. It is important that pastors teach the principle and requirement of submission to their congregation. A lack of submission from subordinates in ministry creates a dangerous climate within the local congregation. Many individuals are motivated by position. These are positional leaders. They see everything through the lens of position. Therefore, it is very easy for them to conduct *acts of submission* without having the *heart of submission*. This must be discerned by pastors. Positional leaders find it difficult to blend in with the congregation. Positional leaders are not content with anonymity and lack of visibility. They are intent on working their way up and into the top tiers of leadership. Therefore, they will find a way to get as close as possible to the top tier of leadership in hopes of "breaking-into" high level positional leadership.

Many positional leaders are looking for a platform to release their gifts, and others are simply too narcissistic to remain in the *ordinary class of believers*. Positional leaders can rarely engage *heart submission* to pastoral leadership, because their secret belief is that their gifts are "equal to" or even "greater" than the pastors they are called to serve. It is not unusual for positional leaders to break Spiritual Protocol years before they physically leave a ministry. They may continue in "acts of service and obedience", but they have no tolerance for the very average and ordinary pastors they begin to see as a result of their close proximity. For these leaders, the relationships that were once awe-inspiring have become ordinary.

Pastors should be very careful about prematurely releasing individuals to positions of responsibility. Too often, we release such 'positional leaders' to assignments, and then must remove them once discovering that they do not have a heart for pastoral vision; rather, their allegiance is *to having their own way*. Often, leaders are attracted to pastors, because of their anointing. However, these same leaders have no commitment to the greater vision of the house, nor do they have any connection to love and support the pastors on a personal level. These leaders are easily detected, because *they cannot be corrected. They make very little emotional or personal investment into supporting pastoral leadership, yet they covet the pastor's visibility, anointing, and authority.*

Most leaders are eager to obtain positions of subordinate authority, but most have difficulties remaining in their ordained position of heart-felt support of their set leaders, discovering that submission is not an easy condition to maintain over extended periods of time. Why is this? It is human nature to devalue that which you become *familiar* with. My once prized Zanotti pumps are now sitting on my closet shelf untouched. After my initial purchase of the shoes I am not as mesmerized as I was initially (although I still treasure them and love peeking at them, as they sit on the shelf in the closet). This is what happens to leaders as they gain greater and greater access to their pastors. What was once considered exhilarating and life-changing encounters with our leaders, have somehow become ordinary moments and memories we put on the shelf.

Sonship

Sonship is a critical phase of growth in the life of a believer and candidate for potential ministry leadership. The Bible speaks of Fathers and sons. Sonship is non-gender specific in spiritual matters; therefore; sonship is inclusive of women called with high appointment in the Kingdom of God. Sonship is a time in which God chooses to prepare the spiritual son or daughter for future elevation and promotion. Legitimacy is sealed when sons come up through the ranks under a process and path of spiritual development. This means the son is mentored and under close scrutiny and tutelage of one of greater rank.

Military personnel understand the analogy of rank and order, but as Christians we pretend not to understand. In the military, the individuals of higher rank command when to eat, when to rise, when to dress, when to retire, when to sit down, when to stand, when to speak, and when to be silent. Soldiers understand that they are in a process of training and development designed to prepare them for dangerous, difficult, and life-threatening military operations. Soldiers understand that they are in a war and must be taught how to fight, how to use weaponry, and how to manage a potentially dangerous arsenal. Soldiers must remain teachable. Soldiers understand that no matter how they are challenged, they do not have time to whine, complain, and become offended, since they must keep their eye on the fight that is sure to come.

In the Kingdom of God, sons are under strict and divine orders. Sons keep the bigger picture plan of God before them at all times, and are able to separate their personal issues from the greater vision. Sons can be lovingly corrected by Spiritual Fathers and Mothers and understand that they are sent to sit under the tutelage of one greater *to learn the ways and mind of God.* Correction by loving spiritual parents amounts to sound counsel and guidance, and is not to be understood as abusive in any way, shape, or form. Only true sons can be corrected. If a leader under a pastor cannot be corrected or redirected by his pastors, then he is not a son. The leader *that cannot be corrected* is an individual that may enjoy the church, but is not connected to a process of spiritual development or guidance. Or this may be an individual who covets the pastors anointing, but is not connected to his pastor's heart. Spiritual sons understand that knowledge has the potential to make one prideful, but experience in a process of sonship is what matures someone for high appointment in God's Kingdom. They discover that God's way is humility, faithfulness, loyalty, and servant-hood. The Bible has much to say about the correction of sons:

"My son, despise not the chastening of the Lord; neither be weary of his correction:" (Proverbs 3:11)

"Correction is grievous unto him that forsaketh the way: and he that hateth reproof shall die." (Proverbs 15:10)

"Correct thy son, and he shall give thee rest; yea, he shall give delight unto thy soul." (Proverbs 29:17)

"O Lord, correct me, but with judgment; not in thine anger, lest thou bring me to nothing." (Jeremiah 10:24)

"For whom the Lord loveth he chasteneth, and scourgeth every son whom he receiveth.

If ye endure chastening, God dealeth with you as with sons; for what son is he whom the father chasteneth not?

But if ye be without chastisement, whereof all are partakers, then are ye bastards, and not sons." (Hebrews 12:6-8)

"Obey them that have the rule over you, and submit yourselves: for they watch for your souls, as they that must give account, that they may do it with joy, and not with grief: for that is unprofitable for you." (Hebrews 13:17)

Sons endure tests which are designed to prove them, strengthen them, and mature them in the faith. God's testing is His way of proving novices, ultimately weeding out the authentic from the counterfeit. Novices are beginners who become lifted in pride after serving for a short period. Novices have knowledge of scripture without wisdom or experience. Novices can be dangerous. Therefore, God will take the novice through a series of tests over a number of years – the pride test, the loyalty test, the money test, the humility test, the faithfulness test, the test of endurance, and the test of offense in an effort to prepare the son for greater use in the Kingdom of God:

"And thou shalt remember all the way which the Lord thy God led thee these forty years in the wilderness, to humble thee, and to prove thee, to know what was in thine heart, whether thou wouldest keep his commandments, or no." (Deuteronomy 8:2)

God cannot use the arrogance, pride, and secret insubordination we offer up to Him. The idea is to pass the test *and not to opt out of the testing session* by running out and starting a church on a whim, leading unsuspecting people astray. This seemed to be the pattern in our experience. There were individuals who were attracted to the anointing on our lives, and therefore sought after close proximity to us as their pastors. They coveted our anointing, but chose to rival us personally. Individuals can love your anointing and despise you *all at the same time.* I describe this as a reversible coat. On the one side of the reversible coat is admiration, but if the coat is ever turned *inside-out*, there you will find envy.

My husband I and have been in Christian ministry all of our adult lives. I became a pastor's wife at age 22 and Bishop was 24. We began in a traditional Baptist setting, but prior to that we were both Spirit-filled, tongue-talking, gonna-change-the-world young people with a vision simply to serve God. We sought to enter ministry without any financial consideration whatsoever. As ministry veterans with medals of honor to prove it – we have seen it all. We have dealt with parking-lot prophets, charlatans, counterfeit ministers with counterfeit anointings, Pentecostal playboys, and false brethren. We have seen intercessory leaders rival us and individuals obsessed with me, emulate me in unhealthy and destructive ways. We have had to ask toxic individuals to find another ministry to poison. We have had to deny false prophets a platform. We have had to address disloyal leaders who wanted to maintain strong ties with disgruntled leaders who had left our ministry in anger. We have suffered betrayal and disconnection with people we have loved and served faithfully. We have faithfully kept the confidences of those members who needed us in hard times, but our faithfulness has not always been rewarded. Through it all, with heavy Apostolic and Prophetic government, we maintained order and believed that God would send the help we needed, and through every season God has been faithful.

Offense

"Moreover, if thy brother shall trespass against thee, go and tell him his fault between thee and him alone: if he shall hear thee, thou hast gained thy brother.

But if he will not hear thee, then take with thee one or two more, that in the mouth of two or three witnesses every word may be established.

And if he shall neglect to hear them, tell it unto the church: but if he neglect to hear the church, let him be unto thee as an heathen man and a publican." (Matthew 18:15-17)

We have learned many things about offense in our many years of ministry. Here is the wisdom I have to offer.

1. **Never take on the offense of another church member**. Although they may be your good friends, their anger

with the pastor or whomever has nothing to do with you. Save yourself a lot of headaches, pain, and family suffering by letting your friends know that you will pray for them, but you are not comfortable listening to negativity about your pastors or any other leaders in your church. Create a distance with these individuals. You cannot forfeit your destiny for your friend's issues.

2. *Never follow an angry man.* (Proverbs 22:24) Never follow a disgruntled member who leaves a church in anger to start another church. Anger is a dangerous emotion. Do not address important destiny decisions in anger. Wait until you cool off and settle down. Take a week or two to pray and meditate on the Word before you make decisions and cast unfair judgments upon people you are in covenant with. Once the dust settles, you will be able to see a thing more clearly and are then better able to act in counsel and sound judgment.

3. *Never discuss an issue you have with your church with co-workers, unbelievers, or another pastor.* If there is an issue, then deal with it directly with your pastors. Call the office and set up a meeting to openly address the misunderstanding. By spreading your misunderstanding to co-workers and family, you are bringing the church under unnecessary scrutiny and

perhaps persecution.

4. ***People who are easily offended are looking for a reason to be disloyal.*** The petty and unimportant issues should not disrupt your peace. If you are not confident in your pastor's leadership, check your level of loyalty first, and if this is not the place, meet with your pastors and remove yourself. But never sit in a ministry and complain and criticize every move your leaders make. If you are not operative in the spirit of love, faith, and faithfulness, you can block your own blessings.

5. ***Never leave a ministry because your disgruntled friend left the church.*** I have seen this happen, and this is unwise and foolish. Never allow friends to suck you into foolishness and malicious and unfounded gossip, because you just don't have the nerve to hang the phone up. *There are some deposits that have a demonic source that you may never spiritually recover from.* These are the dangerous alliances that can have disastrous results, destiny delays, and spiritual destruction. Simply let your friends know that ***you will not entertain foolishness,*** and that your destiny is much too important.

6. ***If there is an offense with a brother or sister in***

the church, by all means seek to resolve it through reconciliation. After you are no longer angry, ask to meet for the purpose of explaining the offense and offering reconciliation and a resolution to the conflict. If this does not occur, then you ask that an elder or minister meet with you both to assist in bringing the issue to resolution (Matthew 5:23, 24, 18:15-17). Never spread a private conflict through *the telephone ministry;* the Bible condemns this type of behavior as *sowing discord (Matthew 18:15; Proverbs 6:14, 19).*

7. *There are some situations that can only be resolved through a parting of ways.* A believer is under no obligation to continue a relationship that is not based in truth. If the offending party cannot deal *equitably or truthfully* it is acceptable to disassociate with those individuals. Every attempt at peaceful and loving resolution should be made. However, in the Matthew Chapter 18 text, there is an acknowledgement that some attempts at reconciliation *cannot be resolved.* Once the proper channels have been exhausted, it is up to the individual to amend his ways. If a believer makes the choice to reject accountability, then he or she cannot be forced to change their poor behavior. You then have the right to break fellowship. If the behavior is considered disruptive to the ministry, the pastor has the liberty to ask the offenders to find another place of

worship. The pastor is the only individual responsible for who is allowed inside the fellowship. As a porter, you must understand that the pastor can open the door of the church to invite and/or open it once again to allow disruptive individuals to leave (John 10:1-5).

Oftentimes, pastors have challenges with leaders who are initially excited during a *honeymoon phase* of ministry, but then when those same leaders become disenchanted or discouraged as they continue serving, egos clash and submissive attitudes are abandoned. As in a marriage, the honeymoon period will only last for several years after which reality sets in, and you begin to see the spouse's flaws and weaknesses. It is critical at this juncture that the leaders called to serve their pastors know several things that I will lay out in the following chapters.

God Has Set You In Your Church Because It Pleases Him

"But now hath God set the members every one of them in the body, as it hath pleased him (I Cor. 12:18)."

There is a function and a purpose that you are called to fulfill as you are joined in faith with your pastor and congregation. The relationship of the pastor and congregational member is likened unto the marriage covenant. There are stages of growth and development. As in any marriage, flaws and weaknesses are exposed, but forgiveness, grace, and love must be present on both sides. None of us would be married today if we divorced the first time we became really angry or even livid about something. Careless remarks, negligence, and simple human error would send all of us heading for divorce courts if this were the case. Not only would the above-mentioned scenario be unreasonable, this would be unstable in a marriage situation. However, what is described is an accurate picture of believers who break covenant with two and three churches within a short number of years. Believers often abort their assignments prematurely and head for the hills after a disagreement with another member, a church policy, or a misunderstanding or offense involving pastoral leaders.

You have been sent into your congregation to grow, to develop, to learn, to exercise your gifts, to give, to sacrifice, and to become an integral part of a larger vision. This takes vision, commitment, and a level of unselfishness. Even as having a successful marriage means staying the course and working-out the challenges of life - so it is in ministry. Fulfilling the calling and appointment on your life will mean staying the course, remaining faithful to your assignment, rejecting offense, and knowing that God has set you in that particular ministry, because it pleases Him. Without the exception of instances of abuse, if the spiritual climate in your church is a healthy one, stay and grow from your experiences.

EVERY BELIEVER IS FLAWED, INCLUDING YOUR PASTOR

"For all have sinned, and come short of the glory of God (Romans 3:23)"

When you find the perfect church let me know, ok? Your presence in the church means it is not a perfect church, because you are not perfect, the pastor is not perfect, and none of the congregants can claim that prize. For some reason, we tend to place our leaders in superhuman status, and when their flaws are revealed, we become angry, critical, and prideful. Why is there grace for the pew and not for the pulpit? Pastors take the members' flaws, failures, and sins to their grave, but the pastor is often the subject of harsh criticism, gossip, and often scandal, because of their high status and visibility.

When leaders have close proximity to pastoral leadership, they must keep in mind that their pastors are flesh and blood human beings *who do not glow in the dark",* as Apostle Ron Carpenter would say. Pastors and Five-fold Ministry leaders have hurts, disappointments, difficulties in their families, money problems, health challenges, and situations where their hearts are broken by members who abuse the trust their pastors placed in them. Pastors are by no means perfect, and their personal lives do not always line up to the utopia we expect. They are anointed, however their anointing must be separated from the individual. Pastors should be respected and honored, because of 1) the anointing and assignment on their lives and 2) because of the ordained office they hold. Even when a pastor acts in a manner that is beneath his or her calling, disrespect is still not an option for the congregational member or anyone for that manner. Spiritual Protocol does not allow a member to correct a pastor. The pastor cannot be counseled or corrected by a member, so any attempt in this regard is *out of divine order.* This is why the pastor has a pastor or bishop. The private matters of life and discipline are addressed by higher authority and not by the congregation, no matter how sincere. The congregation has the duty to faithfully pray for their set man and woman of God; a failure to do so for the congregation is sin, according to the Book of I Samuel:

> *"Moreover as for me, God forbid that I should sin against the Lord in ceasing to pray for you: but I will teach you the good and the right way. (I Samuel 12:23)*

ALL MINISTRIES HAVE WEAKNESSES AND STRENGTHS

> *"And he said unto me, My grace is sufficient for thee: for my strength is made perfect in weakness… Therefore I take pleasure in infirmities (weaknesses), in reproaches, in necessities, in persecutions, in distresses for Christ's sake: for when I am weak, then am I strong (2 Cor. 12:9a-10, emphasis mine)."*

There is a myth that the five-thousand- member and larger mega-church is the prize of ministry. The myth goes on to suggest that the pastors of mega-churches are more anointed, more holy, and more gifted than others. We are further deluded into thinking that these individuals have what they have, because they have "*more faith*" than the pastor of the two-hundred member church in the rural setting. Well, this is just not true. Mega-church pastors should *not* be given demi-god status, they are not a super-human breed, and they are not operative in a superior level faith. They simply have a unique and important, yet difficult appointment. Their ministries are larger, and the truth is that their headaches are larger too. The fact is that these ministries are riddled with different types of challenges, hard to resolve problems, and are under tremendous media scrutiny. The internet has these pastors under heavy scrutiny, and if they stub their toe at the barbeque it is permanently recorded on the internet. I am truly not hating; I am in prayer for many of them, and I respect their ability to remain operative under such unbelievable pressure.

The fact of the matter is that often believers have fantastic ideas about mega-church pastors, and this can often translate into behavior where they begin to *devalue* their own pastors, comparing their pastors and their ministry with the one with all the bells and whistles. Spiritual Protocol requires that the pastor of the local church be held in high-esteem by the congregation, no matter the size of the congregation or the challenging circumstances. There should not be anyone in Christian ministry that the member does not esteem more highly than their own shepherds. This is authentic Spiritual Protocol. Believers must understand that all ministries have strengths and weaknesses. It is very common for ministries to have difficulties with leadership, with administration, with finances, with maintaining membership, and the list goes on. This happens in all churches, and in large mega-churches on a grander and therefore more complex scale.

> *"And we beseech you, brethren, to know them which labour among you, and are over you in the Lord, and admonish you;*
>
> ***And to esteem them very highly in love for their work's sake****. And be at peace among yourselves." (I Thessalonians 5:12, 13)*
>
> *"And I will give you pastors according to mine heart, which shall feed you with knowledge and understanding." (Jeremiah 3:15)*

YOU ARE NOT SENT TO RIVAL, INVESTIGATE OR CORRECT YOUR PASTOR

"And it came to pass, as he had made an end of speaking all these words, that the ground clave asunder that was under them: And the earth opened her mouth, and swallowed them up and their houses, and all the men that appertained unto Korah, and all their goods." (see Numbers 16:1-33)

Korah was a rebel in the camp in the wilderness. God had appointed Moses, his set man, but Korah resisted Moses' leadership and egotistically began to have secret meetings against pastor Moses. Korah managed to gather a group of rebels against the ordained leadership and began to openly challenge Moses' authority. Well, God had an answer for Korah and everyone who gathered against Moses. He instructed Moses to gather them together and to prophesy their demise and when Moses did that, the ground opened up in the form of an earthquake, and Korah and all of his cohorts lost their lives. (Numbers 16:32-34)

It is very important in matters of Spiritual Protocol that God's position is clearly understood. God is not, nor will he ever be on the side of rebellious individuals who seek to rival pastoral authority, to secretly plot against, or investigate their pastor. To investigate your pastor means that you go digging into private areas that do not concern you. This too, would be a breach of Spiritual Protocol. Meetings about the pastor without the pastor's knowledge are illegal meetings, and sincere Christians should not have any part of any such evil. God considers any attack against a pastor a flagrant affront to His well ordered Kingdom. Even if you disagree and feel justified in your anger or disappointment, even if the pastor is dead wrong and *in need* of correction, this cannot come from a congregation member. This would come from a higher authority.

It is dangerous to join a group of rebels, because spiritual offense is contagious. This means that it is very easy for an individual to take on the offense of another and they ultimately forfeit their God ordained destiny. I have seen this happen. Individuals become offended about things that do not directly affect them and they lose it all. Notice in the Numbers 16 text that not only were Korah and his conspirators destroyed, but their wives, children, and possessions. This gives us an indication of the grievous effects of rebellion, and how not only are the rebels adversely affected, but the destiny of their entire family is *permanently altered.* When you are in a church environment, *stick with your pastors,* be wary about siding with disgruntled others. Before you go storming out of a ministry, think about how your children feel about it and how this will ultimately affect their development.

YOUR GIFTS DO NOT SUPERSEDE THE AUTHORITY OF YOUR PASTOR

"And God hath set some in the church, first apostles, secondarily prophets, thirdly teachers, after that miracles, then gifts of healings, helps, governments, diversities of tongues (I Cor. 12:28)."

God has a divine order in mind when he assembles the local church. Divine order means that there is a set spiritual ranking of authority. God begins by selecting a set man and woman, and gives them dominion (Gen. 1:26) in a city, region, or an even greater territory. The man and woman God selects is called to an ordained office. According to Ephesians 4:11; God has ordained the Five-Fold offices to serve as governing offices in the Body of Christ. The office represents a spiritual dimension of power, as well as it represents great anointing upon a chosen individual. These offices give structure and stability to the local assembly. Without these advanced offices, there would be no local assembly as we know it. Individuals are *not* placed in office, because they win a popularity contest or because they are attractive or smart. They assume office, because they possess the anointing and the unction to function in such capacity. Five-Fold then becomes the foundation of a local assembly.

After Five-Fold Ministry, God adds gifted individuals who strengthen the hands of the set man and woman. These individuals are normally highly anointed and intelligent, accomplished, and full of ministry capacity to fulfill the mandate upon the house. We have such individuals in our midst, and it is a joy and an honor to serve them in the pastorate. However, it is important to the understanding of Spiritual Protocol to note that according to I Corinthians Chapter 12, spiritual giftedness does not trump spiritual ordained office. Therefore, no matter how gifted an individual may be, their gift does not make them *superior to the pastor*, nor does it make them *more anointed* or *more qualified* than the set man or woman. This is an important matter in Spiritual Protocol, because often gifted individuals come into a local church and because they can preach heaven down, the perception may be that their pastors should now provide them a platform for their ministry. This would be out of divine order. When God calls a Five-Fold pastor, that set man and woman have *the total* responsibility for the ministry and have no obligation to turn over anything to anybody. The set man and woman are the only individuals called to the pulpit of that local assembly, so they are under no obligation or requirement to give anyone the microphone to say anything unless directed by the Lord. Therefore, leaders with *a lust to preach* and *a lust for visibility* and spiritual greatness should check their ego at the door when entering an Apostolic House.

YOU ARE CALLED TO PRAY AND TO COVER YOUR PASTORS

> *"And Shem and Japheth took a garment, and laid it upon both their shoulders, and went backward, and covered the nakedness of their father; and their faces were backward, and they saw not their father's nakedness (Genesis 9:23; see v. 20-29).*

Spiritual Protocol requires that a congregation connected in covenant with their pastors cover their pastors in constant and vigilant prayer. The spiritual attacks against high ranking Five-fold gifts are nothing short of alarming and wide-spread. There are spiritual assassins and religious henchmen waiting to pounce on any weakness, failure, mislabeling, or discrepancy of disgruntled others against your shepherds. In this hour, pastors and ministries are operating under unprecedented scrutiny and strain. The higher the ranking of the leaders; the more vicious the attack. Somehow, members jumping and shouting forget the reality of spiritual warfare surrounding their pastors and forget the vital importance of praying for those that feed them. The same *prayerless* members who are yet jumping and shouting all over the church remain oblivious to the heinous attacks launched against their pastors, *and* are the same ones who would be the first to leave the church and scandalize their former shepherds if the ministry becomes unglued at the seams.

Prayer is a cover for your pastors in the spirit realm. In the Book of Genesis, we find a drunken Noah whose flesh, the Bible says, was *uncovered,* and the man of God was in need of assistance. The Bible says that Noah's son Ham looked upon the nakedness of his father; left him uncovered, and then told others (his brothers). But Noah's sons Shem and Japheth walk into the tent backward showing *deference and reverence* for their father, and covered his nakedness with a proper garment, *never looking upon his flesh* and they were blessed for their deed. Ham was in grievous violation of spiritual protocol. Ham failed to reverence his father, peered into Noah's private places, *and then spoke of it openly.* When Noah awakened he cursed Ham, his youngest son, because he should have reverenced his father, even in his father's apparent exposure and sin. This is why Ham was cursed. Ham was not cursed because of his skin color as the Fundamentalist Bible-toters would have you believe. Ham was cursed, because he failed to obey *Spiritual Protocol.*

NEVER LEAVE A CHURCH WITHOUT THE BLESSING OF THE SENIOR PASTORS

"And Esau said unto his father, Hast thou but one blessing, my father? bless me, even me also, O my father. And Esau lifted up his voice, and wept."
(Genesis 27:38)

It is important when operative in Spiritual Protocol that an individual never leaves a ministry without the blessing of the Senior Pastors. The Book of Genesis details the importance of securing the blessing at critical junctures in the lives of the sons of the patriarchs. The blessing was such a critical prophetic pronouncement that Rebekah helped Jacob to scheme to obtain the blessing from his old and infirmed father Isaac. Esau disregarded the blessing and devalued it to the degree that he sold it to satisfy his flesh and the Bible says, *"... Thus Esau despised his birthright (Gen 25:35)."* The birthright is what positioned one legally to receive the blessing that would come at the time of the son's maturity. The blessing was of supreme importance to the degree that the patriarchal blessing was *coveted*. Anything that was coveted by the patriarchs should be thoughtfully considered:

1. The blessing was so important that the positioning

(the birthright) for the blessing was contested, and Esau sold it to Jacob.

2. The blessing was so important that Isaac rose from his deathbed to pronounce it prophetically over his son.

3. The blessing was so important that Rebekah conspired against her own husband to have it spoken over her youngest and favored son.

4. The blessing was so important that in Genesis 49, Jacob rises from his deathbed to give the commanded blessing to all twelve of his sons.

If the blessing was valued and contended for in the lives of the patriarchs of old, why isn't the blessing contended for today? I assert that a lack of understanding and teaching on Spiritual Protocol is what allows so many to fall into spiritual confusion and the trick of the enemy. Before a Hebrew son could leave a house, he had to wait for his father to give the blessing. The commanded blessing was the spoken and prophetic impartation that sealed the past season and opened heaven over an individual for the commencement of adulthood or the new season. It is a prophetic and reverentially spoken command.

Pastors have the spiritual authority to speak this blessing over sons and daughters who have done well as it relates to faithfulness, loyalty, and the fulfillment of assignment. When members leave a church in heated disagreement or offense, it closes the door for the pastors to address the offense, heal wounds if needed, and then declare the blessing. This is the gross error that many fall into repeatedly. If there is a misunderstanding, meeting with your pastors before you leave the ministry would give your pastors *an opportunity*, at a minimum, *to respond to* whatever grievance or misunderstanding you may have. Authentic men and women of God would be pleased that their members respected them enough to meet with them before they chose to leave their ministry. In my experience, anything as vital as leaving a ministry should not be done in haste. God is not in a hurry to do anything. At a minimum, wait until you calm down, allow your anger to subside, and then make a decision. Judgments made in anger and haste are *never* sound judgments.

The Jethro Principle And Spiritual Protocol

*E*very pastor needs significant others to assist him in carrying out the vision. It is unimaginable that God would appoint a set man and woman to launch a work and provide them no assistance, encouragement, or support. Sometimes because of pride, arrogance, or lack of understanding, a pastor may try to do it all, particularly in the early stages of ministry. However, every pastor soon discovers that he or she does not possess all the talent, skill, or physical strength to accomplish the entirety of the vision without skilled help and delegated authority.

Pastor Moses was very skilled and dedicated; however, he was using a model of ministry that excluded delegating authority to others and releasing them to assist in serving the people. After a visit from Jethro, Moses' father-in-law, Moses implemented a model for ministry, called *The Jethro Principle*, which included 1) leadership training and 2) delegated authority.

"Hearken now unto my voice, I will give thee counsel, and God shall be with thee: Be thou for the people to God-ward, that thou mayest bring the causes unto God:

*And thou shalt **teach them ordinances and laws, and shalt shew them the way wherein they must walk, and the work that they must do.***

*Moreover thou shalt provide out of all the people able men, such as fear God, men of truth, hating covetousness; **and place such over them, to be rulers of thousands, and rulers of hundreds, rulers of fifties, and rulers of tens:***

And let them judge the people at all seasons: and it shall be, that every great matter they shall bring unto thee, but every small matter they shall judge: so shall it be easier for thyself, and they shall bear the burden with thee." (Exodus 18:19-22)

Jethro instructed Moses to choose significant others who would be qualified to rule, and who would help him bear the enormous burden of ministry. This model of delegated authority is used in most corporate entities - secular, religious, and military. The Jethro Principle is a model of leadership training and delegated authority. Leaders cannot be released without proper training, and all delegated authority has limits and boundaries that it cannot cross. Leaders should know what to handle and that there are some cases that are beyond their jurisdiction and need to be brought to their pastors.

The Jethro Principle and model of leadership delegation can only function properly within the context of Spiritual Protocol. Delegated authority must understand that its authority is always conferred and never assumed. Elders, ministers, and others under pastoral authority must be aware they are guests in *another man's house*, and their behavior should reflect this. One of the qualifications for promotion is that one shows himself faithful in another man's house and with another man's vision. We want our own churches, ministries, and followers, but first we must be found loyal, faithful, and diligently working under the authority of others without comparison, criticism, contention, competition, or covetousness.

"And if ye have not been faithful in that which is another man's, who shall give you that which is your own?" (Luke 16:12)

When Delegated Leadership Rebels

THE CASE OF MIRIAM

Miriam was a tremendous ministry gift. She was Moses' sister and a Prophetess. By all accounts, Miriam was highly gifted, a prophetic psalmist, and probably preacher and singer – a triple threat. She and Aaron served as Moses' inner circle and advisers in the camp and therefore she had high influence and visibility. The fact that she was recorded at all in the Old Testament is evidence of her tremendous leadership role amongst the Israelites. In spite of her great anointing and status, Miriam defied ordained leadership. The Bible says that Miriam and Aaron spoke against Moses, because Moses had married Zipporah, an Ethiopian woman (Numbers 12: 1). This is indication that spiritual leadership can become quickly carnal in many instances. Carnal leadership cannot be governed, since they have cast off the leading of the spirit and have opted for soulical leadership in which the individual is now being governed primarily by their emotion and egotism. Moses is leading a major movement of God, and his critical leaders decide to concern themselves with fleshly and unimportant issues:

> *"And Miriam and Aaron spake against Moses because of the Ethiopian woman whom he had married: for he had married an Ethiopian woman.*
>
> *And they said, Hath the Lord indeed spoken only by Moses?* **hath he not spoken also by us? And the Lord heard it…**
>
> *With him (Moses) will I speak mouth to mouth, even apparently, and not in dark speeches; and the similitude of the Lord shall he behold: **wherefore then were ye not afraid to speak against my servant Moses?***
>
> *And the anger of the Lord was kindled against them: and he departed.*
>
> *And the cloud departed from off the tabernacle; and, behold, Miriam became leprous, white as snow: and Aaron looked upon Miriam, and, behold, she was leprous.*
>
> *And Aaron said unto Moses, Alas, my lord, I beseech thee, lay not the sin upon us, **wherein we have done foolishly, and wherein we have done foolishly, and wherein we have sinned…***

And the Lord said unto Moses, If her father had but spit in her face, **should she not be ashamed seven days?** *let her be shut out from the camp seven days, and after that let her be received in again. (Numbers 12:1, 2, 8, 9, 10, 11, 14)*

Leaders serving under delegated authority need to understand several things:

1. **No matter how great your gifts and contribution, God speaks to and sides with His set man and woman** (Numbers 12:5-9).

2. **Carnality and inflated ego will get you in trouble with your leaders and with God.** Stay out of messy mess. Shut it down. Don't listen. Hang up the phone. End the conversation (Numbers 12:1-2).

3. **Miriam was the ring-leader and received the harsher punishment.** The scripture indicates that *Miriam and Aaron* spake against Moses. Miriam, the more dominant one, is listed first in this account. Aaron was pulled into messy-mess by Miriam the one with the stronger personality. Leaders should be careful not to allow other leaders to pull them into foolish behavior in the house of God. Leaders should be careful never to take on someone else's offense or issue (Numbers 12:1).

4. **Leaders should be aware that *God is listening*,** even to conversations they think are private. God is often offended by private, critical, and foolish speech that leaders often engage in one with another behind the backs of the set man or woman of God. In the case of Miriam, after God heard the offensive speech, He immediately *"came down in the pillar of the cloud"* to deal with the issue of insubordination (Numbers 12:5).

5. **It is foolish to come against God's anointed, even if you feel you have just cause (Numbers 12:11).**

6. **Miriam paid a consequence for her violation of *Spiritual Protocol*** (Numbers 12:10,15).

7. **God took Miriam's offense personally (Numbers 12:14).**

THE POSTURE OF DELEGATED AUTHORITY IS THAT OF SUPPORT AND PRAYER

Israel is in the midst of intense warfare against Amalek at Rephidim. Joshua is down in the valley fighting and Moses is on the top of the hill *with the rod of God* in his hand. The rod of God is the instrument of Intercession. This is the same rod that parted the Red Sea. The miraculous occurs when Moses has that rod of Intercession in hand. This is an indication that there is a supernatural and numinous component to intercession:

> *"And it came to pass, when Moses held up his hand, that Israel prevailed: and when he let down his hand, Amalek prevailed.*
>
> *But Moses' hands were heavy; and they took a stone, and put it under him, and he sat thereon; and Aaron and Hur stayed up his hands, the one on the one side, and the other on the other side; and his hands were steady until the going down of the sun.*
>
> *And Joshua discomfited Amalek and his people with the edge of the sword." (Exodus 17:11-13)*

The Ministry of Intercession is critical to overcoming spiritual attacks and advancing Kingdom of God territory. Without the ministry of intercession, battles cannot be won, territory is lost, and divine protection is forfeited. Lasting and effective redemptive work cannot be achieved and sealed, until the effective Ministry of Intercession, both private and corporate is engaged consistently through delegated leadership. Ultimately, leaders should be trained and skilled in interceding for their pastors and local church ministry. When Pastor

Moses could not keep his hands lifted in prayer, Aaron and Hur were needed to step in and keep Moses in a posture of prayer, necessary for victory. A ministry can stagnate, lose momentum, and forfeit territory, because leaders fail to engage in corporate intercession. The text helps us to clearly see that supernatural progression and intercession are vitally linked. One cannot manifest without the other! Prayer is a supernatural act with gloriously supernatural outcomes!

God is looking for delegated leadership that is mature enough to accept the call to pray forcefully, and to command the blessings of God over set leadership. Oftentimes, we hear of great ministries falling apart. This is as much a responsibility of the set leadership, as it is of those called to serve and support the ministry. Rather than choosing to gossip, God is looking for leaders who will take up the mantle to pray for their pastors and other leaders who endure intense seasons of battle and attack.

How To Care For Your Man And Woman Of God

1. ***Your pastors need your prayers and support.*** Lift them up continually and faithfully before the Lord. When you pray for your family, needs, and concerns, don't forget to lift up the man and woman of God and their family. Lift up their family, their finances, and their Kingdom mandate and assignment.

2. ***Your pastors need your words of encouragement.*** Don't forget that a hug, a note of inspiration, or a kind email goes a long way to encouraging your pastors. It is amazing to me that members somehow want to be inspired, but fail to reciprocate the inspiration they receive. Make sure that you are not in the group that never comes up to greet your pastors after service. It is important that you give hugs and/or send an email, or note of inspiration. If you are a woman, never fail to greet and encourage the woman of God, while you are

greeting her husband.

3. *Your pastors need you to celebrate the Word they minister.* Not only should you celebrate the Word, you should study it and meditate upon it throughout the week. After your pastors minister the Word, they need you to honor the Word that was preached without analyzing it. Simply say, "Pastor that was an awesome Word this morning!" Nothing further is necessary.

4. *Your pastors need you to find ways to connect with them.* If they lead small group events, such as Sisterhood or Brotherhood Ministries, these are events you should attend as a show of support. Also, if they are asking for participation in events that include travel, this is a way to show love and support. If you are invited to a special private event by your pastors, then you make it your business to be there. If you are invited to their home, bring a small gift as a token of gratitude. This is etiquette and a show of honor.

5. *Your pastors need you to refrain from gossip intended to harm them personally, their children, or other ministry leaders.* They need you to defend them and the church when malicious slander is brought to you. They are counting on you not to feed into and spread nonsense.

6. **Your pastors need you to honor their marriage**.
This means that you are not to honor the one and
dishonor the other. There is no organizational position
or administrative office that is sandwiched in-between
the set man and the set woman of God. God is not
into dividing couples. The spirit of *religious tradition*
has successfully separated the sexes, and over the years
pastoral marriages have suffered as a result of this.
The separation and dividing of the man and woman
of God has a satanic source (Matthew 19:6, Mark 10:
9). Your pastors come as a couple and a package deal.
They function as one. The set woman only answers
to her husband and no one else in the church, and
there are no positions or individuals operative to
divide this unity. All women in ministry and females
in administrative capacity come under the set Woman
of God *as a daughter*, and serve at her pleasure. Rivals
and competitors are out of order. Hagar has no place in
the house. Women who cannot assume *the posture of a
daughter* may not be assigned to your ministry.

7. **Your pastors need you to sow sacrificially into the
ministry and into their lives personally**. It is expected
as a member that you consistently tithe and give
offerings (Malachi 3:8-12). Also, your pastors need
you to sow sacrificially into their lives when you are
personally impacted by their revelatory teaching and

impartation. Sowing seed or giving sacrificially is a way to honor your pastors and to acknowledge that there is a supernatural exchange taking place (I Corinthians 9: 11-14, 2 Corinthians 9:6-10; I Samuel 9:6-10).

"And he said unto him, Behold now, there is in this city a man of God, and he is an honorable man; all that he saith cometh surely to pass: now let us go thither; peradventure he can shew us our way that we should go.

Then said Saul to his servant, But, behold, if we go, **what shall we bring the man?** *for the bread is spent in our vessels, and there is not a present to bring to the man of God:* **what have we?**

And the servant answered Saul again, and said, Behold, **I have here at hand the fourth part of a shekel of silver: that will I give to the man of God, to tell us our way.**

(Beforetime in Israel, when a man went **to enquire of God***, thus he spake, Come, and let us go to the seer: for he that is now called a Prophet was beforetime called a Seer.)*

Then said Saul to his servant, Well said; come, let us go. So they went unto the city where the man of God was." (I Samuel 9:6-10)

Spiritual Protocol For Pastors

1. **Be careful who you give close proximity.** Find individuals who are worthy. When the disciples looked for homes to lodge in they would seek out *worthy individuals.* Believers full of ego and *the need* for high visibility may not be the best choice.

2. **You cannot produce or maintain momentum with the wrong leaders in place.**

3. **Have an outlet of vacation time and fun with your family as often as possible.**

4. **You cannot always trust what people say, just watch what they do.**

5. **Non-tithers cannot handle God's money for it is holy unto the Lord.** All counters and money handlers

should be faithful in tithes and offerings.

6. **Never give an individual a second chance to be disloyal.**

7. **When a leader becomes too familiar, he will begin to speak inappropriately, address situations that do not concern him, and behave in a manner that reveals his secret sense of entitlement.**

8. **Don't be afraid to remove individuals from positions.** Oftentimes, leaders can stagnate in a position if they are there too long. To keep their vision and skills fresh they may need a change of focus. Sometimes leaders need to be removed from position for acts of insubordination or for the greater need of the ministry, and sometimes because they have become territorial or complacent.

9. **Keep private matters private.**

10. **Watch for individuals who join your ministry for a platform to showcase their gifts, and not to serve the greater vision.** *Lay hands suddenly on no man (I Tim 5: 22)* means that pastors should *not* promote individuals prematurely.

11. **Reward humility and reject the proud** (as God does). *Watch for the 5 C's of pride - comparison, criticism, competition, covetousness, and contention.*

12. **Do not promote individuals who cannot receive your patient, loving, and constructive correction (Hebrews 12:7-11; 13:17).**

13. **Spiritual authority is released in a congregation through teaching/preaching. If the wife of the pastor has no teaching/preaching opportunities, then she has no authentic spiritual authority or influence within the congregation.** If a pastor is serious about partnership, then he will promote and release his wife's gifts to the congregation more than several times a year.

14. **The wife of the pastor must be presented to the congregation by the pastor as a partner in life and in ministry.** This means that her role and line of authority must be clearly defined. The pastor must present her assignment to teach/preach/administrate and he must clearly articulate his full confidence in her ministry and put his full weight and support behind her. *This cannot just be a feeling or idea of the pastor – this must be articulated and presented to the congregation if the wife is to be honored and respected.*

EVERY PASTOR NEEDS SPIRITUAL COVERING

Every pastor needs a pastor. There needs to be some significant individual(s) in your life that you can go to for private counsel, guidance, and sound ministry strategy. The problem is that many pastors go about doing ministry without the proper level of support, prayer covering, and wisdom that experienced Spiritual Fathers and Mothers can bring to the table. Too often, pastors are trying to reinvent the wheel. Too often, pastors are attempting to do too much or too little.

Often, after investing tremendous amounts of mental and emotional energy into the ministry, a pastor becomes weary, burnt out, and often wounded by saints within the house. Who is to minister to the wounded pastor? Who is there to listen to the challenges and the heartbreak Pastors face? Where can a pastor go to unpack his personal issues in a safe non-judgmental environment? The pastor keeps the congregation's confidences, but who keeps the pastors confidences?

When my husband and I entered the ministry in the late eighties, we had no idea what we were in for. We had no idea of the extreme highs and lows of ministry, the betrayals, the lean seasons, or the unforeseeable challenges involved. We just had a burning desire to serve God. We had no clue about spiritual attacks, or the manner in which they would come. All we had was a vision and an anointing from God. We had no Bishop or significant other to speak into our lives, and the few that attempted to assist us did not have the revelation or experience to help us at all. It was a lonely and difficult walk balancing home and ministry as a young couple in our mid-twenties. It was so difficult in fact that looking back in hind-sight, we probably should have waited some years before entering full-time ministry. Nevertheless, God had a divine plan, and in this season a part of our assignment is to do the following:

1. To nurture and to support pastors in difficult traditional assignments.

2. To aid pastors who are transitioning out of traditional models of ministry into the Kingdom paradigm.

3. To promote healthy and successful Apostolic and Prophetic church launches.

4. To promote healthy spiritual partnerships between husbands and wives called to the pastorate.

My husband and I oversee the Living Waters International Alliance (LWIA), which is a powerful network of churches and para-church ministries designed to strengthen and release dynamic Apostolic and Prophetic ministry in the Twenty-First Century. It is our mandate to equip and train leaders for cutting-edge, Kingdom of God strategy, resulting in church growth and professional leadership development. As overseers with the anointing and gifting for oversight, our assignment is to establish supportive relationships with pastors, which will in turn produce empowered and successful ministries.

ADVANTAGES OF JOINING AN APOSTOLIC NETWORK OF CHURCHES

1. Promote and encourage your calling and vision as pastor.

2. Provide sound strategy for church growth, administrative, and leadership development.

3. Cover the private issues and concerns of marriage and family.

4. Provide prayer, logistic, and administrative support when needed.

5. Provide a rich fellowship of like-minded pastors who are launching Apostolic and Prophetic Ministries.

6. Offer a blueprint and a pattern for Apostolic and Prophetic Ministry.

7. Offer revelatory teaching in the form of Conferences and Summits. Our Living Waters International Alliance offers the premier Apostolic and Prophetic Conference in the nation, called *The LWIA Conference,* held at the Destiny Center in Newport News, Virginia each January. Also, my husband Bishop Steven W. Banks and I host *Apostolic and Prophetic Summits* in various locations around the nation.

8. Offers opportunities to engage global Apostolic teams and humanitarian missions to foreign nations; thereby, expanding the reach of the pastor and the local church.

About the Author

Dr. Keira Taylor-Banks and her husband Bishop Steven W. Banks are the Senior Pastors of Living Waters Christian Fellowship of Newport News, Virginia. She is a distinguished and uniquely anointed female leader, preacher, prophetic teacher and visionary. With profound insight into the Kingdom of God, Dr. Keira is a sought after and highly favored ministry gift speaking nationally and internationally.

Dr. Banks is the co-founder and overseer with Bishop Banks of the Living Waters International Alliance, an international network of Apostolic and Prophetic churches and ministries. She is the founder of the Lily Housing Corporation, an international charity established to provide transitional housing for women with children. Dr. Banks has served as host of various shows for the Trinity Broadcasting Network (TBN) from the Virginia Beach studios and is the executive producer and host of her very own inspirational television show, *No Limits with Dr. Keira Banks* broadcasting from The Destiny Center. She is also the author of the groundbreaking works, *The Matriarchal Dimension* and *The Prophetic Dimension*.

Made in the USA
Middletown, DE
13 May 2019